A Lost Empire

Robert Herschbach

Ion Books
P.O. Box 111327
Memphis, Tn 38111-1327

An Ion Chapbook
Ion Books
P.O. Box 111327
Memphis, TN 38111-1327

Library of Congress Cataloging-in-Publication Data

Herschbach, Robert, 1966
    A lost empire / Robert Herschbach.
      p.   cm.
    ISBN 0-938507-23-0 : $7.50
    I. Title.
    PS3558.E7598L67 1994
    811' .54--dc20
                                 94-33668
                                 CIP-

Acknowledgements

The author wishes to thank the editors of *100 Words* and *Quarterly West*, periodicals in whose pages poems in this chapbook have appeared.

Special thanks to: Angela Ball, James Galvin, Jorie Graham, James Kimbrell, Katherine Ouzts; Alissa and Elisabeth Herschbach; my grandparents, Michael and Alice Pittas. And Suzi, *ti voglio bene*.

Cover Illustration © Nancy Clift Spicer
Chapbook Design by David Spicer and Nancy Clift Spicer

For My Mother and Father

Contents

Raw

The dog part of me hankers after its buried bone.
The leash part of me feels the pull
      of the color brown, like a siren in the trees.
And the hand that would guide, how many fingers?
And the cold that would snap them up
      if I pulled off my gloves to show you
      the "m" in my palm, as if I were part of a message...
It will never be unscrambled. Evil will never get us
      to dance in a circle, even though Mephistopheles
      is making the rounds in the guise of a dog-like
      happiness.
All day I've been feeling the urge to smile, as in the face
      of a pistol.
I threw out the vat of fermenting locusts. I cut off the ear
      that was making me sin.
I took off my mourning hat, I put on the umber coat.
I wore the ochre pants.

My name is Raw. Did you see me, rising out of the mud?
I saw you, pulling the coin from under your tongue
      to buy a croissant.
They will not be fooled, you cannot mortgage your death
      for food, not when work is the measure of days
And the earth is no longer
      the door to a secret room where darkness churns,
      but is warm paint to lie down in, your hair fleshing out
      the empty spaces.

To the mud on your boot, I offer my broken tooth, as proof.
To the cream of your neck, I offer my forked tongue, as a spoon.
To the hazel in your eyes, the mole on your left breast, I say: compadre!

By Train

The more things move,
The more I am at the center
Of a diminishing kingdom.
Anchored to the seat

Like a tsar on a gilded
Throne, I raise the plastic
Cup to my lips and drink.
That much is certain.

The Physical Evidence

Your fingers unhook
And let drop (moist
Palm) and you watch it
Spin (cold lips) into
The charged atmosphere.

It is a smudge. It is
An aphid stuck to the fine
Blue page. You can flick
It off, but it is a mole
On a delicate cheek, that
Draws you in, fascinated.
It is the loud tie, missing
Button, the one black sock
And the other that gives you
Away. And yes, the bellhop

Was smirking. And yes,
The young soprano felt it too,
Her breasts heavy against
The gauzy fabric, a small pool
Of sweat spreading across her
Front as she tried to raise
Herself into the zone of pure
Music. And eyes kept aiming
Their gravity at her until
She had shrunk to the size
Of a moth, you kept staring
With your snake head and your
Five tongues until she turned
To stone. Then you were left
Holding the score of Wagner's
Liebestod. Tenderly your fingers
Ran across the surface, notes
Pinned and mounted like insects.

How you would like to efface
Such wounds! Would restore
The ecstatic blankness
Of the staves, then gently
Peel them off also.

An Epic

My liege, this is a brittle place.
Cortez, with his excellent nose
Sniffing out no scent of gold
Would surely have passed it over.
And the dogs pawing at tubers,
The pink bellied dogs

Mounting each other from boredom...
The sky like lacerated flesh.
We went to the creek,

Which was heaving up fish. They were
A marvel, for they had no eyes or scales,
But were rubbed into pale, indeterminate
Shape. They fell apart in our hands.
And my liege, he said: find the red root.
And six of them held me down, reached
Into my mouth. And my liege, he said:
Find the magic acorn. And he held
The penknife to the soft, pink flesh
Of my ear, and I was afraid.

And he said: do not fear, for we are all
Blessed by the golden hands of the sun.
And he held up the ear, like a moist fungus.
Look how nature has blessed us, he said.

———

Cortez, his face like jagged rock.
His shoes, two slabs of blackened
Meat, breaded with dust. The equation
He carries in his head
Like "Country Roads." It goes

Something like this: if *x* is the modest
Wingspan of days, and *y* cramps us
Into its nook, if the bigger half
Of a wishbone equals the better part
Of mercy, if the number of stones
Weighing me down shall determine
How quickly I learn to swim,

Then what use dreaming

———

Of cool terraces, of bare feet
On marble? And the well fashioned
Sandal? And the wicker chair
To act as a frame

For constantly shifting thighs
And bellies, intertwining laughter?
Sticky as a damp sheet was the air.
The moon like a huge vitamin,
Undissolved

In the night's throat.
My long hair like a curtain.
He opened it, and my face
Was bald in the halflight,
A lump of white putty.

His fingers pulled back
The sleek cords, in his hands
My head was a rounded globe
On which he traced cities,
Canals. Do not fear, he said,
We are all

Already absolved, even now
Somebody's clammy fingers
Are sponging the page...

What Are You Afraid Of?

Someday I'm going to wake up
And not be able to see
Out of my eyes, which are stone,
Or move my hands, which are fish.

The barbed wire caught in my lip.
The skin washing ashore like sheets
Of plastic. And the tin can
In my head, empty.

One of these days the Jew's harp
In my throat will snap, just as I thought
I finally had it—the answer

To the Sphinx, and the other riddle
Where legs are strings,
And we fiddle.

Pavane

The marble ear listens to water.
Rain, rain and the pigeon's feathers.

The ink runs
Like laughter. The children return

To the flesh that bore them, shrinking
To the size of a walnut,
An oyster's pearl.

The city flexes its asphalt limbs.
The black cabs gleam

Like woodworms. Burrowing into
The rotted trunk to unearth
Sweet sap. But the odor smothers.

The house must be fumigated!
The frayed sofa, its dog hairs
And licorice, consigned

To the fiery furnace. "That is where
Your mother and I first held
The small kernel of desire

In our palms and watched it grow
Into an unyieldy plant, requiring
Special tablets and plentiful

––––––––

Water." It drips from branches
Onto the bald head

Of the bust in the garden.
It shoots through punctures
In the rubber hose, spraying

The legs and thighs of muddy
Children, but laughter
Is waterproof. No one can contain it,

Or the accrual of moisture
On the high ceilings, the puddles
Taking shape in the basement, seeping

Into the foundations. An arterial
Pipe bursts, the city floods

With hard hats and curiosity
Seekers. The leaning tower
Slips one inch further

Towards the muck, goldfish
Wriggle like souls above
The tarnished coins

———

In the slimy basin, beneath
The pigeon-encrusted nose
And eyeless stare

Of the god of the fountain,
The listening ear.

The Shape Of An Onion

Because it is pure white, you cannot see
What stalks the letters. It is moving. Time
To put on the rubber suit, cock the harpoon
and fire. "A life

Of earnest contemplation," to find oneself
Impaled on a spike–as one's feet, wet
From ritual, come into contact with wire.
Jimmy claims it was a Vatican plot.

Agua hermetica was in the ink they used
To illuminate the manuscripts, prolonged exposure
Leads to watery eyes, dissolution of fingertips.
A burning in the throat, to be followed by choking. *God*

I miss you, and the electrodes
Attached to my gonads, to jumpstart the body
Into self-flagellatory ecstasy. For what
Would we not endure that our sky might be

A rod or a cone in the divine cathode?
And that we practice on each other in your absence,
And the fatted calf abandoned, bleeding, and Polynices
Tonguing the dust where he fell, his brother's wound

Festering in him, so that you might take offense
And visit us in form of weather, wind
That is more than wind...

———

"A life of earnest contemplation," scanning
The wind for possible syllables, telegraphy
Out of the white noise like wave-spray.
Or staring at the page in hope

16

The beast will stare back
From behind the cage and emit
Frightening yowl, proof of the need for poetry.

————

My life, like an onion, is clarified by what sizzles
On the other side. Time to put on the rubber suit
And dive into the funnel, for here is a whirlpool
At the very heart of contemplation, to find

Proof of the need for poetry. Can you not feel, man?
The teeth, I mean, the invisible teeth, and dissolution
Of fingertips. But they are still here, I can see them.
Yes, but are numb. Pressing the keypad,

But transmitting no syllables. More than anything
I want to attain that state of grace the instant
Before skin, wet and conducive, touches.
Moreover, the ink I use

To illuminate these letters, i.e., to heighten
So that they burn greenly in the mind, is toxic
In a subtle way, so prolonged exposure chokes.
I keep wanting to finish, it is stupid

To want to finish, for I am *a man of no fortune
And with a name to come.* Destiny is to fall
Drunkenly from the rafters into the threshing machine.
There will be no eulogy, there will be no bronzed trophy,

But a burning in the throat, followed by choking.
Better, I think, to act out dismemberment on the page
As a stay against the frightening yowl of that beast. The cage

————

Is all that's between us. We have been chasing each other
Around for hours, now—who has enough decency
To surrender? For time, it hath a cruel harpoon,
It maketh no clean wound, but festers in the blood,

Turning thoughts to crimson, like sick counsel
Of some Rasputin, staring palely at the queen in hope
Of access. Meanwhile, snap, crackle of bones

Against flagstones. We have bunions
To remind us of history. We have the potted plant
On the windowsill to remind us of pastoral poetry,
For which there is a proven need

No longer. Jimmy claims it was a Vatican plot,
But what does Jimmy know, festering in the tower
In which we are all imprisoned, implicated
In the conspiracy

To anoint Polynices with *agua hermetica* and jumpstart
His gonads into ecstatic spasms, beckoning forth thousands
Of flagellatory selves to penetrate the rubber suit
And gas mask of the future,

For what would we not endure that we might be
A rod or a cone in the hypercritical eye of the future?
We practice on each other in its absence.

————

A man of no fortune, and with a name to come.
Call me Ishmael—here is my cruel harpoon,
At your feet, milady. Call me Rasputin.
Here is my long nose and blistering stare,

Cataracts. Because they are pure white,
I cannot see what stalks the empire, though it is
Moving. In the privy chamber, a fatted calf
Tonguing our bunioned feet, we sit and dream up

Proof of a need for God, so we might hold
The frayed cord to his skin. When it toucheth,
Shall be frightening yowl,
Shall be poetry.

Purity

Not for all the tanks in Russia,
My sweet, would I abandon
Your thumbnail, or the blue vein
In your onionskin wrist.

Not for the bald stare
Of a demigod, or marble fingers
That hold the threads and make
The music cohere, would I extract

The gold tooth from your mouth,
Or cut the long braid to fashion
A scaffolding, though the muck
Is up to our knees and rising,
And others, more buoyant, swim
In glassy air above us.

Look at their clean toes.
Look at their legs, struggling
To stay aloft.

Souvenir

Don't forget the camellias,
She said, or the tongue in your mouth
That turned to glass

When you tried to speak, that dissolved
Into water. You want to swallow
The past like a capsule, spreading
Ink through veins

Of a leaf until you are marble.
But camellias, and the serious look

Of an eight-year-old practicing piano scales.
And girls in the courtyard, singing
"Princess Tatiana." Never forget
The stem, the stake in your heart
That pins you forever.

————————

The scent was of lemon trees,
But how you would like to believe
It was their voices, transmuted, picked up
By the breeze.

————————

Don't forget the ghost of a smirk haunting
The courtesan's face

In the mosaic, as if to say "They jailed me
Here–how about you?" Or the bare feet
Or sandals of those who walked in the above
World, Constantinople, A.D. ____ You

Who listen to rustle of leaves and hear
Tambourines, or booty of coins, or sea,
Do not forget the medallions that made
Holy the wrist of Madame, her finespun soul,
Circumscribed by no time or place, staring
At you from inside the painted cage
Of her face. *Learn to inhabit the split seam
Of what and why,* she said,

Placing the cards face down on the table.
You turned one over, and there you were,
Leapfrogging into the sun. And there
You were, nailed up to the sky with stars.
Never forget, she said, *what night heals,
Day reopens.* And the muezzin,

Climbing his minaret
To rub salt in it.

―――――

As if the sky were a wall
To listen against for voices
On the other side, arguing
About us,

Our plans for the future.
As if the piano keys were Scrabble,
And the points were chalk
On a face that turns away
So what we see

Is wood. It takes work to visualize
The canals on Mars. You have to stretch

Your imagination like a muscle
Until it hurts, and ignore
The urgent telegrams

Of *cease and desist,* bending
Your voice, like a muezzin's, to "cry
Of its occasion." It takes practice
To summon up the ghost

Of a smirk on the face
Of Princess Tatiana, doubled up in a pit
With her yellow hat and her dog,
Even if you hold hands and dance
In a circle, in the courtyard,

And the scent is of lemon trees.
As if the earth would wear us
Like a chemise, patterned
With camellias.

As if we could collect the debris
And broken glass and recycle it
Into piano scales, or a mosaic
In which a courtesan

Brandishes a tambourine against
What contains her, as if to say
Don't forget.

Sundown

Because my feet know where the ground is, I thought
The clay and bits of stone must be my inheritance,
And that the wildflower, being red, marked the spot
Where he, whose bones are under

My skin, spat out his final offer.
Because my kneecaps are quiet, I guessed they are still
Listening for a reply, or even an echo. Still, that I am thinking

Now is a kind of reprieve, if not an absolution, for Iphigenia
Spoke proudly to the assembled armies, but her last words
Were to the cicadas. Their response ceases and begins as the sky reenacts
The climb up marble steps to the blade that rose like a moon
Above the altar. *Goodbye, sweet light.*

———————

No one wants to shut the fuck up and drive the car.
No one wants to be married off to a hero whose secret name resounds
       in the caverns and cisterns, in the void between stars.
Brothers, sisters, should I compare you to broom
       that pigments the rise and fall of a stony landscape...
       are you really so wild and predictable?
No one wants to be predictable.

When I have thrown out all that is not my own, there will be no ears
       so please do not disturb my present listening.
When you come to retrieve my stolen goods please do not bother
       the rightful owners, they are happy

Hoarding their trunks
       of dust. What is left
       of their golden souls is wooed
       by sunlight.

I should have had those other hands, with the long fingers.
I should have had piano lessons.
And now you want to blame my nose for taking the shape
        of the fruit it loves most.
Not figs, not dates, not the moist body
        of a cicada, not even color
In the abstract sense, which is the hungriest.

I should have had eyes in my toes, to bring me closer.
I should have put on the winged sandals, but I gave them to you instead,
        and now I have to watch you flail

        all over the page, too far
        out of earshot for me to warn you–arrows, the king's men...

————

Shear off the rest of the hair, and leave me alone
With my name. *We will perfect*

                                        its pronunciation.

Burgeoning on the brave stem like a flag, my head
Is a broadcast, that infiltrates your house
Like aromatic spring, and your muscles,
How do they respond? Emptiness

–a light that blinks on a tower, to warn you
That what was there

                        you might still crash into

*Wife, why do my legs, like roots, soak up the purple
Carpet?* But these are not words to live by, but marks
On a tongue I stick out at you–no one

Can feel the press of my brain against its new skull,

No one can possibly know the life
Of blind fish

in underwater caves.

Drunken Orion, the rush of wind is a sign
Your arrows

Have missed us again! But if I am still,
And resist your curious stare, it is that I am busy
Becoming aware of the head
As it melts

Into the heart. Guide your eyes back
To your own sockets, darkness and see
What constellations are there for me
To personify?

———

Because green was the lizard, I thought
It had a flag to raise. Because the kernel
Stuck in my throat, I thought water...but it was not water
But retsina we were drinking, that tasted of pine

And led us to thinking of landscape, how it may be
Imbibed, that it stick to the veins like a claim
For a particular

Plot near a shrub or an olive tree whose shade
I can enter and say I know the history of

Iphigenia.

Witness

Leo, Pisces, Gemini...fire, fire, fire.
I thank them for keeping their distance.
Hardness within, hardness without.
Stone, and bone. We sit, leaning back—
Orion! The belt of Orion is fire, his body is
Distance. And the lines are busy, the callers
From each of the nerve centers have urgent
News for the brain. The steps,
Older than us, flaunt their hardness.
We are still porous, but learning to be
Unsentimental in the face of a planet's
Downsizing. I thank them for keeping me
On, and promise to waste no more paper
On fanciful extrapolations of weather,
But to get to the news in the least words
Possible, like the nightjar. It was summer,
We heard it over and over as we witnessed
The meteor shower in Orion, in Greece,
And felt how hard the steps were,
Compared to us, who were just learning
Endurance. Now it sticks in my mind,
The recollection of a nightjar

That is now an idea. As for "Orion's belt,"
It is a peephole into a hunger that keeps
Its distance, the lines are busy with calls
To come closer, the calls are tendons,
The body glows. Virgo, Taurus, Aries,
Aquarius...